THE
RESILIENT
WOMAN

What It Means To Be Resilient; How To Build
Resilience & Why Resilience Is Important For
You To Overcome Life Challenges Plus Amazing
Stories & Perspectives!

Written By

PASTOR FLORIS S LYMON

CONTENTS

DEDICATION

To myself: I feel the need to celebrate myself unapologetically, for not giving up even when the going got tough, when it felt like I just could not take it anymore, through days of breaking point, when it felt like I was progressing, then suddenly! It looked like a setback was showing up, for holding on, for self-determination, for the spirit and strength to persevere, not being ashamed when help was needed at any given point in time, for continually looking after and serving both family and community, not only when it was comfortable, for the experiences gained through every challenge, lessons learnt and the growth I have personally attained as I walk through life's journey.

My late Mum: Words are not enough to describe this great woman of strength, dignity, integrity, and honour. I acknowledge the great work she carried out in her life time to nurture not only five of us as her children, but many other children she picked from the streets, ensuring they got their education until all dispersed into various spheres of life. I admired the way she fought and pulled through the dirty politics and manipulation in her teaching profession; also in her service in the religious sector. She did not forget her cool and calm disposition as she faced death while battling a terminal illness. My Mama deserves the best accolade!

My daughter: This pretty young teen has just blossomed in my eyes, amidst various challenges, including losing her dad at a very young age.

She definitely had her moments of "highs" and "lows." I admire every bit of her strength and how she deals with unpleasant events (such as dealing with peer-on-peer conflicts, friendship issues, bullying, etc.)

She just knew how to support me when I had my lowest moments; her courage and strength to carry along with me regardless has always been spectacular. She is practical in diverse ways, blessed with various skills that she self-taught, learning from one mistake to the other, and not allowing failure to deter her; that also is phenomenal!

My Lady D, you are indeed a young, resilient woman!

Every resilient woman: For every time you have been stretched and pulled like a rubber by various life unpleasant events, then manage to put yourselves together again; Kudos to you! It is never too late to recover. Remember! Your processes are different. What matters is that you still put yourselves together at the end of each event or challenge.

INTRODUCTION:

—⁘—

How Did I Get To Choose This Title?

In the month of March 2021, Mother's Day was celebrated across many countries in the world. I was asked to minister at my local Assembly to celebrate and acknowledge mothers and every woman who has the responsibility of looking after a child or children.

My topic was "Five Main Characteristics of a Resilient Woman." I went in not fully prepared, as it was a last-minute decision. However, I decided to give my best, and to my amazement, this is the fruit of that seed planted in March 2021. "A Book"

I finished the session, but I started feeling like there was a lot more to say, coming to think of how women get through various challenges in life and still manage to run the home, look after children, do their various businesses, multi-tasking on various levels, going to work, and the list goes on and on. So straight away, I knew there was an opportunity for me to elaborate further on this. The strangest and weirdest thing was that my Pastor was thinking the same from his end. He wasted no time but to send me a voice note with feedback on the session I had, and also at the end of his message was: "I think you can write a book about this. There is a lot more to say about the subject matter." That just further confirmed what I was thinking in my heart; I could do more justice to the topic.

Drawing from my first experience of writing two years ago, it started in a similar way, having dealt with a topic and then receiving feedback about putting it into writing. Once I start hearing this, I have learnt not to waste time. In fact, It opens the door for me to start thinking and having a flexible mind into various ideas about the subject matter. I must say obedience is one of the keys to success. We can also add sensitivity and listen to the good judgement of others.

In April 2021, I started jotting ideas, reading more about the subject, and having conversations with a few women around me and with some men, including my son, who is now nineteen; I call him "My young man." Smile!

It's amazing how everyone got hooked up with the conversation. I had to remind myself, saying: "hold on, Floris! You are a resilient woman too." Then I started thinking about my entire life's journey and how far I have come, definitely by the Lord's special grace. Below are some remarkable events that stretched me to the core as the years went by:

A disappointment from a relationship I held so dearly in 1992, the claimed prosecution of my father for treason, found guilty and awaiting death by hanging on the gallows; this happened around 1997 – 1998, when my country Sierra Leone was still suffering the effects of the war it had already endured for many years. Then, I was already in University; I went through emotional, psychological, and social trauma. It was tough; no way to further describe it. Hmmm! I nearly dropped out, but bless my beloved mother. May her soul rest in perfect peace.

Another major event happened in 2009 when I lost my husband, leaving me with two very young children. They were six and four years old at that time. Oh my God! My world turned upside down. I never knew I would get through. I never knew what it meant to be a single parent. I was not ready. I had to learn a whole new pattern of living. Well, as we would normally say: "the rest is history." By his special grace, I have made it this far. Events of my life as a single parent and how I have survived so far, can be found in my first book titled: "Don't Judge Me I'm A Single Parent."

I often ask myself this question: How did I get here? "Boy o Boy"! Have I been stretched more than an elastic band? Have I been pulled to the left, right, centre, and all around? Surely! Did I feel like next to nothing? Yes, on some occasions. Did I seek help and support? Oh yes, indeed! Did I manage to navigate my way through, despite all odds? Surely! by the Lord's grace and from obtaining wise counsel. I'm I still standing? Well, this book tells you so. Hallelujah! Have I learnt a lot? Of course, as experience is one of the best teachers, it can only make me a better person and a stronger one too, as I face the next challenge. Is this all in the past? Not at all! As long as there is life, there will be issues that come to stretch and pull me on a daily, weekly, monthly, or yearly basis.

I recently went through almost a month of stretching, especially with my health. I was not expecting my New Year to start with frequent visits to the hospital, as I was already looking forward to plans and projects to be fulfilled. It felt like a standstill; all I could see was setback, delays, and frustration. I took time off work to rest while waiting to fully recover and just to take things slowly. However, I challenged myself, my faith that I will ensure I do everything that was necessary to get better, I mean spiritually, physically, emotionally, etc.

In my weakness, I tried to hold on to hope, and I looked out for the positive outcomes in the situation upon reflection, the joy and satisfaction I had, after checking myself in, which was a great action I took, also being grateful to my Lord for the facilities provided by the Health Care Services, which adds value to life. I hung on to my grip and never let go. I fought the battle of the mind with the help of the Holy Spirit and through the spiritual and physical support gained from loved ones in the faith. I have realised that the spirit of resilience continues to grow day by day, as we encounter the pulling and stretching of life and overcome them one after another.

Again, whenever I talk about these life processes, it always takes me back to my late mother, on how she had pulled through in life amidst all odds until she met her demise. She was a woman of substance who was proud of her strengths and also accepted her weaknesses. A woman who sustained provocation while studying for her master's degree at age 62, she was still pursuing education alongside her children.

Sadly, some folks just cannot fathom such a scenario. She almost dropped out of university after two major losses in the family, my late husband and also my aunt, who was a first cousin to my mum, a beautiful gem with whom I was very connected. The gap between both deaths was very short, and this left a huge emotional and mental impact on my mum. How she managed to finish her course, and not only finished, but with "flying colours," a 2.1 as one could describe it, was another huge encouragement to the family.

While he was in jail, a wife, who stood and fought for her beloved husband, accused of "Treason," was already condemned to death and awaiting death by hanging over the Gallows. Words are not enough to describe my phenomenal mother. Indeed! Her resilience has inspired me greatly.

I could vividly remember how I have seen and heard about many other women who have fought their way through in life, talking about women in politics, housewives, the professional and business arena, women in ministry, and women who pulled through war-torn countries, to name a few.

Following from what has been said above, I believe you can agree with me that this is worth writing about as every woman will relate to this, not only women, but also young girls and boys raised by both older and younger women, and also men who were raised by biological or non-biological mothers, married men, men with female relatives, or men working with women in any given environment or the society in general, can attest to the fact that women have that thing called "Resilience" in them to a certain extent.

This is not to undermine our fantastic men out there, but having to come to the realisation that it should be recognised about women, and it is fitting to give "praise where it is due and to whom it is due," then it is fair enough to engrave this strength on the women. We all can attest that our men and boys have their level of resilience too. However, on this occasion, I encourage us to be truthful and jog our minds, think about the women around us, in no particular order, from mothers, friends, fiancés, wives, workmates, sisters, aunties, cousins, etc.; on how you have seen them pulled through significant or day to day events in life, how they have influenced you with their strength and resilient spirit, and what makes you qualify them as resilient if you were put on the spot to describe a resilient woman you know.

THE AIM OF WRITING THIS BOOK

To acknowledge and celebrate every woman, both young and old out there, for allowing resilience to be built and developed through life's journey.

To encourage every woman to draw their source from other women around them, be inspired to face and conquer the day-to-day challenges of life.

To encourage sharing stories of resilience that will uplift and deliver others who feel less hopeful about coming out of particular situations.

To inform and encourage that we are all winners, having fought through one situation or the other, whether big or small.

To encourage us all that resilience is a process, and therefore everyone's pace can be different. We must work with our diverse paces, find solutions that suit particular situations and work with them.

We are encouraged to seek help when we are struggling and cannot help ourselves. Inviting others into our lives to help us should never be seen as a sign of weakness but a display of strength and resilience.

To know that, even when things seem to be falling apart, you can tap into that reservoir of capacity inside of you to enable you to keep yourself together.

Take a seat, relax and enjoy as you read along.

Chapter One

DEFINITIONS OF THE WORD "RESILIENCE"

———————✦✧✦———————

The Miriam Webster dictionary defines the word in two ways as follows;

1. The capability of a strained body to recover its size and shape after deformation caused especially by compressive stress.

2. An ability to recover from or adjust easily to misfortune or change.

The "Very Well Mind" Article, posted by Kendra Cherry on the 24th of April 2021, states that: Resilience is what gives people the psychological strength to cope with stress and hardship. It is the mental reservoir of strength that people are able to call on in times of need to carry them through without falling apart.

In an article by the American Psychological Association in 2012, psychologists defined resilience as the process of adapting well in the face of adversity, trauma, tragedy, threats, or significant sources of stress, such as family and relationship problems, serious health problems, or workplace and financial stressors. As much as resilience involves "bouncing back" from these difficult experiences, it can also involve profound personal growth.

Another Article, namely "Everyday Health.com," updated in December 2020, defines resilience as the ability to withstand adversity and bounce back from difficult life events.

As we can all see and read from the above, there are lots of similarities amongst all definitions. We identify words like; recover, bounce back, strength, adjust and withstand.

A general mind-tickling task for us all; Just think about as many instances you can remember, how you have fought your way through by bouncing back or drawing from that extra reservoir of strength when needed most.

As much as this book celebrates the resilience of women, I believe everyone has had their time of recovery one way or the other. Even babies, infants, and teenagers have been observed for pulling through some situations that adults would not necessarily withstand. Obviously, there might be several factors responsible for that, such as age which is a major one to consider especially when dealing with ill health or certain medical conditions.

In my course of reading and studying, I bumped into some quite interesting Articles on gender-related resilience research.

I also discovered that there are different types of resilience, namely:

Emotional Resilience: There are varying degrees of how well a person copes emotionally with stress and adversity. Some people are, by nature, more or less sensitive to change. How a person responds to a situation can trigger a flood of emotions.

Emotionally resilient people understand what they're feeling and why. They tap into realistic optimism, even when dealing with a crisis, and are proactive in using both internal and external resources. As a result, they can manage stressors and their emotions in a healthy, positive way.

Psychological Resilience: Psychological resilience refers to the ability to mentally withstand or adapt to uncertainty, challenges, and adversity. It is sometimes referred to as "mental fortitude."

People who exhibit psychological resilience develop coping strategies and capabilities that enable them to remain calm and focused during a crisis and move on without long-term negative consequences.

Physical Resilience: Physical resilience refers to the body's ability to adapt to challenges, maintain stamina and strength, and recover quickly and efficiently. It's a person's ability to function and recover when faced with illness, accidents, or other physical demands.

Research published in April 2016 in *The Journal of Gerontology* showed that physical resilience plays an important role in healthy aging, as people encounter medical issues and physical stressors.

Healthy lifestyle choices, building connections, making time to rest and recover, deep breathing, and engaging in enjoyable activities all play a role in building physical resilience.

Community Resilience: Community resilience refers to the ability of groups of people to respond to and recover from adverse situations, such as natural disasters, acts of violence, economic hardship, and other challenges to their community.

Real-life examples of community resilience include New York City following the 9/11 terrorist attacks; Newtown, Connecticut, after the Sandy Hook Elementary School shooting; New Orleans following Hurricane Katrina; and the communities of Gilroy, California, El Paso, Texas, and Dayton, Ohio, in the wake of mass shootings, July bombings in London, and the August Mudslides in Sierra Leone where I originate from, to name a few.

I believe we can all agree that nations became more resilient in the face of the recent COVID-19 pandemic. The resilience of nations has been tested, but not for a very long time like this before.

Chapter Two

FACTORS OF
RESILIENCE

H ere is another great source found in the Everyday Health Article as I continued my study. It claims as follows:

Developing resilience is both complex and personal. It involves a combination of inner strengths and outer resources, and there isn't a universal formula for becoming more resilient. All people are different. While one person might develop symptoms of depression or anxiety following a traumatic event, another person might not report any symptoms at all.

A combination of factors contributes to building resilience, and there isn't a simple to-do list to work through adversity. In one longitudinal study, protective factors for adolescents at risk for depression, such as family cohesion, positive self-appraisals, and good interpersonal relations, were associated with resilient outcomes in young adulthood.

While individuals process trauma and adversity in different ways, there are certain protective factors that help build resilience by improving coping skills and adaptability. These factors include:

- **Social Support** Research published in 2015 in the journal *Ecology and Society* showed that social systems that provide support in times of crisis or trauma support resilience in the individual. Social support can include immediate or extended family, community, friends, and organizations.

- **Realistic Planning** The ability to make and carry out realistic plans helps individuals play to their strengths and focus on achievable goals.

- **Self-Esteem** A positive sense of self and confidence in one's strengths can stave off feelings of helplessness when confronted with adversity.

- **Coping Skills** Coping and problem-solving skills help empower a person who has to work through adversity and overcome hardship.

- **Communication Skills** Being able to communicate clearly and effectively helps people seek support, mobilize resources, and act.

- **Emotional Regulation** The capacity to manage potentially overwhelming emotions (or seek assistance to work through them) helps people maintain focus when overcoming a challenge.

Research on resilience theory shows that it is imperative to manage an individual's immediate environment and promote protective factors while addressing demands and stressors that the individual faces. In other words, resilience isn't something people tap into only during overwhelming moments of adversity. It builds as people encounter all kinds of stressors on a daily basis, and protective factors can be nurtured. (Everyday health article)

The 7 Cs of Resilience

We now take a look at the 7 Cs of Resilience, also found in the everyday health Article. This model was put together by a certain Paediatrician Ken Ginsburg MD, who specializes in adolescent medicine at the Children's Hospital of Philadelphia. He set up this model to help kids and teens build the skills to be happier and more resilient. However, adults can benefit from it too!

The 7 Cs model is centred on two key points:

- Young people live up or down to the expectations that are set for them and need adults who love them unconditionally and hold them to high expectations.

- How we model resilience for young people is far more important than what we say about it.

- This article also features a summary of the 7 Cs by the American Academy of Paediatrics as follows:

- **Competence** This is the ability to know how to handle situations effectively. To build competence, individuals develop a set of skills to help them trust their judgments and make responsible choices.

- **Confidence** Dr. Ginsburg says that true self-confidence is rooted in competence. Individuals gain confidence by demonstrating competence in real-life situations.

- **Connection** Close ties to family, friends, and community provide a sense of security and belonging.

- **Character** Individuals need a fundamental sense of right and wrong to make responsible choices, contribute to society, and experience self-worth.

- **Contribution** Ginsburg says that having a sense of purpose is a powerful motivator. Contributing to one's community reinforces positive reciprocal relationships.

- **Coping** When people learn to cope with stress effectively, they are better prepared to handle adversity and setbacks.

- **Control** Developing an understanding of internal control helps individuals act as problem-solvers instead of victims of circumstance. When individuals learn that they can control the outcomes of their decisions, they are more likely to view themselves as capable and confident.

We can see that the 7 Cs of resilience illustrates the interplay between personal strengths and outside resources, regardless of age.

Medical Doctor Amit Mood was also featured in this Article. He describes Resilience as "the core strength you use to lift the load of life."

Chapter Three

WHY IS RESILIENCE IMPORTANT?

I came across this response by Joshua Miles, BA MSc, published on the 15th of May 2015 in the Counselling Directory UK, and this sat very well with similar thoughts I had.

It reads: "As we all know, when we are in a weakened position where we feel as if things are going from bad to worse, it can be very difficult to find our balance, or swim against the tide, or, recover and regain stability. Resilience is important for several reasons; it enables us to develop mechanisms for protection against experiences that could be overwhelming, helps us to maintain balance in our lives during difficult or stressful periods, and can also protect us from the development of some mental health difficulties and issues."

While we all walk through life's journey, whether young or old, we tend to encounter challenges, from day to day, or some that can be described as very traumatic, such as losing a loved one, financial or business loss, surviving wars, family breakage, marital and relationship issues, job loss, health challenges, or community trauma such as the COVID 19 pandemic. Life can be tough on us sometimes, and for us to get through from one point to the other, as a way of escape or finding solutions, there has to be something inside of us that gives us that ability to want to survive or pull-through/bounce back. Some people have it naturally, but some also have to learn the art of having that thing. It is called "Resilience." How can we overcome without resilience? It takes winning that battle in the mind that we can do it no matter what.

Naturally, we all would just fancy life without any aorta of trouble, issues, etc. We just want to get to that destination without any bruises. However, life has proven to us that it does not work like that. Instead, going through life's challenges and coming out of it with a sign of resilience has a lot more benefit for us and many others around us. I struggled with this notion for years. Romans 8:28 reads: ***"And we know that in all things God works for the good of those who love him, who have been called according to his purpose."*** How can coming out of that situation that looks so negative work out for my good? This scripture verse was one of the scriptures I struggled with, despite my belief in God's word. This verse was quoted to me by my father in the Lord, when I lost my husband in 2009. I will never forget how I felt inside when he read the verse to me. I was so angry in my spirit, man, I felt like asking him out of my house immediately. At that moment, that never sounded right in my ears, despite being a person of faith and knowing that I would have used that same verse to encourage someone else. Then, I just could not figure out how I was going to navigate my way out of life. Hmm! Till now, I do not know and cannot tell how I manage to make it this far. His grace and my willingness to persevere as time went on, hoping and being open to opportunities, helped me greatly. It's weird how it made no sense to me then. But now, I understand much better, as every now and then, I find myself counselling, encouraging, and supporting others who have gone through similar situations. I sit down for a rethink, I then wonder that there is no testimony without a test, no message without a mess, no learning without an experience, and there is no giving outside to others of what we do not have inside. Therefore, we ought to put on that coat of resilience with pride though painful at times, but also comes alongside it a lot of benefits, firstly for self, and secondly for others.

Adding a scriptural flavour to this conversation helps those of us who are believers and how we ought to fight spiritually, physically, and for almost everything that belongs to us, and even when it looks like we are losing, we are admonished to still fight on. Ouch!

Let us take a look at these scripture verses: [10]*"Finally, be strong in the Lord and in his mighty power. [11] Put on the full armour of God, so that you can take your stand against the devil's schemes. [12] For our struggle is not against flesh and blood, but against the rulers, against the authorities, against the powers of this dark world and against the spiritual forces of evil in the heavenly realms. [13] Therefore put on the full armour of God, so that when the day of evil comes, you may be able to stand your ground, and after you have done everything, to stand. [14] Stand firm then, with the belt of truth buckled around your waist, with the breastplate of righteousness in place, [15] and with your feet fitted with the readiness that comes from the gospel of peace. [16] In addition to all this, take up the shield of faith, with which you can extinguish all the flaming arrows of the evil one. [17] Take the helmet of salvation and the sword of the Spirit, which is the word of God."*
NIV

The scriptures remind us that we were never promised a trouble-free life. However, when trouble or any challenging life situation arises, the Father promises us that he will help us either get through or overcome them, having placed our faith in him that he can do so. John 16:33: *"I have told you these things, so that in me you may have peace. In this world, you will have trouble. But take heart! I have overcome the world."* Christ is also saying that, if he overcame what was done to him, we too can overcome by tapping into his grace with faith.

Again, we come across another sighting in the book of Isaiah chapter 43 Verse 2: *"When you pass through the waters, I will be with you; and when you pass through the rivers, they will not sweep over you. When you walk through the fire, you will not be burned; the flames will not set you ablaze."*

Here is another scripture that encourages us about some of the great qualities that come out of our personalities when we endure challenges and how they help us come out on the other end. James chapter 1 Verse 2-4: *"My brethren, count it all joy when you fall into various trials, ³knowing that the testing of your faith produces patience. ⁴But let patience have its perfect work, that you may be perfect and complete, lacking nothing."* **NKJV**

Romans chapter 5 Verse 3-5 reads, *"More than that, we rejoice in our sufferings, knowing that suffering produces endurance, and endurance produces character, and character produces hope, and hope does not put us to shame, because God's love has been poured into our hearts through the Holy Spirit who has been given to us."* **ESV**

Chapter Four

TEN WAYS TO BUILD YOUR RESILIENCE

W hether we are naturally resilient or not, we can learn to develop a resilient mindset and attitude. To do so, we are encouraged to incorporate the following into our daily lives: This is an extract on "developing resilience" from an online article called "Mind Tools."

1. **Learn to relax.** When you take care of your mind and body, you're better able to cope effectively with challenges in your life. Develop a good sleep routine, try out a new exercise or use physical relaxation techniques, like deep breathing or meditation.

2. **Practice thought awareness.** Resilient people don't let negative thoughts derail their efforts. Instead, they consistently practice positive thinking. This means listening to how you talk to yourself when something goes wrong – if you find yourself making permanent, pervasive, or personalized statements, correct these thoughts in your mind.

3. **Edit your outlook.** Practice cognitive restructuring to change the way that you think about negative situations and bad events.

4. **Learn from your mistakes and failures.** Every mistake has the power to teach you something important, so look for the lesson in every situation. Also, make sure that you understand the idea of «post-traumatic growth" often, people find that crisis situations, such as a job loss or the breakdown of a relationship, allow them to re-evaluate their lives and make positive changes.

5. **Choose your response.** Remember, we all experience bad days, and we all go through our share of crises. But we have a choice in how we respond: we can choose to react with panic and negativity, or we can choose to remain calm and logical to find a solution. Your reaction is always up to you.

6. **Maintain perspective.** Resilient people understand that, although a situation or crisis may seem overwhelming in the moment, it may not make that much of an impact over the long-term. Try to avoid blowing events out of proportion.

7. **Set yourself some goals.** If you don't already, learn to set SMART, effective personal goals that match your values and help you learn from your experiences.

8. **Build your self-confidence.** Remember, resilient people are confident that they›re going to succeed eventually, despite the setbacks or stresses that they might be facing.

9. **They believe in themselves,** and this also enables them to take

risks. When you develop confidence and a strong sense of self, you have the strength to keep moving forward and to take the risks you need to get ahead.

10. **Develop strong relationships.** People who have strong connections at work are more resistant to stress, and they›re happier in their roles. This also goes for your personal life: the more real friendships you develop, the more resilient you're going to be, because you have a strong support network to fall back on. (Remember that treating people with compassion and empathy is very important here.)

11. **Be flexible.** Resilient people understand that things change and that carefully-made plans may, occasionally, need to be amended or scrapped.

Chapter Five

SOME AMAZING STORIES AND PERSPECTIVES OF RESILIENCE

#1 The Resilient Woman Perspective From – Oyinlola Bukky Akande

RESILIENT AN IMPORTANT TOOL TO OVERCOME LIFE CHALLENGES

"You may have to fight a battle more than once to win it."
—Margaret Thatcher

To be resilient means that you are a person with the ability to bounce back from defeats, discouragements, or hardships.

No one wants adversity, but everyone gets it. As a follower of

Christ, it is vitally important that we fully embrace the reality that we will experience setbacks, difficulties, and defeats. Some will be serious. These are the situations (even seasons) that will test your resilience in Christ.

The greatest men and women of the Bible were not super-people, but they had great resilience through their experiences and journey of life. There are few people I would like to draw our attention to.

Considering **Noah,** who did not let any challenge keep him from building the ark, by pushing through the negative people and ignoring doubters, Noah got a promise from the Lord because he was resilient.

Quote: *"Do not judge me by my success; judge me by how many times I fell down and got back up again."* —**Nelson Mandela**

Deborah was called upon to lead Israel into battle and was victorious. This woman will challenge you in diverse ways with her determination and a unique character. I am so encouraged by this woman because she was resilient in achieving her goals with the help of God. I must say that part of being resilient is to set and work toward goals. This would lift our eyes off the problems and struggles of each day to an achievable prospect for the future. Staying resilient no matter the circumstances gives you a sense of accomplishment and purpose every day.

Quote: *"That which does not kill us makes us stronger."* —**Friedrich Nietzsche**

Now is the time to set those goals to help you look toward the future with meaning. Be proactive! Build that resilient spirit in you! You are capable.

The faithfulness of the women that followed Jesus from Galilee was worthy of emulation. Despite the fact that the crucifixion of our Lord Jesus Christ, these women were committed and faithful just because they were resilient. They also refused to allow situation and circumstance to take their focus away. **Luke 23 v 55: "The women who had come with Jesus from Galilee followed Joseph and saw the tomb and how his body was laid in it."**

To be Resilient, you will first be required to start with a decision that will help with starting off the race, while the rest of the others will begin to introduce you on the journey.

Must be able to gain and retain attention; I meant it requires a high level of focus and a close walk with the Lord.

The older you become, the more you should expect to grow. Life is a challenge and needs specific tools to overcome it.

Quote: *"I can be changed by what happens to me. But I refuse to be reduced by it."* —**Maya Angelou**

In the book of Genesis 1 v 28, we are required to be fruitful, multiply and replenish the earth, thereby producing results, profitable, and in a position of production and reproduction.

Then God blessed them and said, "Be fruitful and multiply. Fill the earth and govern it. Reign over the fish in the sea, the birds in the sky, and all the animals that scurry along the ground."

When I look back at the different tools that have helped me in life so far by the grace of God, I can confidently say it was the ability to recover quickly from difficult conditions. The ability to get up from a bad situation and begin to live again is the tool that needs to be desired.

Quote: *"We are not a product of what has happened to us in our past. We have the power of choice."* —**Stephen Covey**

Resilience is a very important tool to overcome life challenges and ensure great success. I was taught to be comfortable with rejection and learnt not to fall apart, but to keep going and still put myself out there. So, I learnt to be rejected without it affecting my belief values but seeing concepts to reality. Then one can access and recess oneself and walk into a greater level of success and spiritual growth. I target to be a support or serve my community without being stopped by the challenges of life and create opportunities for people to connect and be financially free.

#2 The Resilient Woman Story - From Master BT

This is about a resilient woman who is now in her 50's. About 20 years ago, she married a guy that she met here in the UK. She originated from an African Country. For the first few years when she got married, it all seemed so good; she was in employment, and her husband also had a job which required him to travel quite a lot. It was a very well-paid job, which was located in a very nice neighbourhood, had a very nice house, and nothing was lacking. By all accounts, the man was very successful, and so was the wife.

The job he had, got him to travel to different parts of the world; so, there were times that he spent most of the month outside of the country, then within it. As a result, he could go for a couple of weeks to America, and on his way to Cairo, or go to Uganda, or to Australia, and finally to China. On a few occasions, his wife will join him, but because of her job, she had to stay in the UK while he travelled around the world.

Everything started to change on this particular day, when by some miraculous stroke of God's intervention, she picked up his phone and saw sexual images of him being very intimate in bed with someone. She was very shocked, and to add to her shock was the fact that the person he was in bed with was a man. She was very surprised, and she didn't know what to do at first. However, she decided to confront him; so basically, after a long-drawn-out issue of confession, the marriage broke up, followed by a great deal of depression. She just lost it, and because she wasn't focused, due to all that she was going through, she lost her job, she left the house where they both lived; she just lost everything. She had to start from Ground Zero. I mean this took years for her even to be able to consider holding down a job because of the depression that she suffered.

She started putting herself back together and began looking for work with support from church and family. She then moved in and was staying with her sister; she had jobs here and there, and sometimes still not enough money. She had to trust God for the basics to assist with her daily living. She stayed with her sister for a while, and then she later found favour and got another place.

However, due to the inconsistency of her earnings, she was unable to maintain her bills.

Yet again, she decided to seek support from her sister by moving in. She felt bad that she had to come back to her sister's, the feeling of staying there for a long while. As a result of this, she would leave her sister's house on some evenings to go to sleep at the airport, because she didn't want to be a burden to her sister. Unfortunately for her, her genuine concerns became a reality, when one day, her sister told her to leave the house because her husband did not find it comfortable for her to be around for such a long while. So, she left without a clue as to where she was going or how she was going to spend the night and the rest of the days to come. She had to hang on to her faith in God; despite having no money, she went out trusting God to direct her steps. She was definitely hoping for an encounter with someone who might be of help to her.

She got on the train that morning. There was a woman opposite her, and she believed that God gave her a word for that woman. She was challenged in her spirit mind as to how that could be possible, knowing very well she did not have a place to stay, which was a priority as far as she was concerned, instead of doing ministry. After battling back and forth, she decided to take the bold step to speak to the lady opposite her.

She said to the lady: "Listen! I believe I have a word for you." She gave the word to the woman; the woman pleaded with her that they should get off at the next station because she wanted to share some things with her as well. They got off at the next station, and the woman confirmed with her that apparently, the words given to her were so accurate that this woman was so impressed with her, to the extent of asking whether there was any chance she could see her at another time. The lady laughed because she didn't know where she was staying that night; she now opened up about her situation, and as a result,

SomeAmazingStoriesandPerspectivesofResilience

the woman said to her: "you know what, you can stay in my house tonight, you are going to be staying with me," and she went home and stayed with the woman and her partner.

She ended up staying with that woman for about 9 months. What an amazing story to tell!

She also told me another story about God's Faithfulness, whereby she had a job interview, the interview was miles away from London, and at that time, she didn't know how she was going to travel to the place. However, she decided she was going to just go on the train. She got to the station, and as she was going towards the barrier, she saw a friend that they all used to go to school with, and that friend, assuming she had the ticket, just opened the gate as they chatted their way through to board the train. As they journeyed on, the train stopped at a station, and then a Train Ticket Inspector got on the train. The inspector asked everybody for their tickets, but when he got to her, he said: "somebody's looking good today"; he was distracted he didn't even ask her anything with regards to her train ticket; he just went to the next person. He said the same thing to her once he came back from the other carriages.

She smiled and told him she was going for an interview. They talked until the train arrived at her stop. She said goodbye, and that was how she made it to her interview. Fortunately for her, she got the job, but was now thinking about how she was going to travel to work, since she had no money yet for a train ticket. Her friend she had met at the station arranged with her that she would wait for her at the train station every morning to open the gate for her to go through to get to her new job. It was also a wonder that no one ever stopped her to ask for one during her journeys for that whole week without a ticket.

During her job interview, she was asked how she wanted to get paid, either monthly or weekly. She responded that she needed to get paid weekly, as she knew in her mind, she would be able to buy her ticket to travel. Indeed! She was able to buy a weekly ticket for her travel to work. Again, she was grateful for a school friend who had appeared all of a sudden to be of help when needed most. Her friend could no longer wait for her at the station.

She finally began to settle down again after seasons of life's challenges. She was also able to acquire her Apartment, having paid for it fully by herself.

Since then, she has never forgotten the amazing grace and faithfulness of the Lord in her life. Today she travels around the world to share her story and encourage many other women.

That is resilience right there. Oh wow!

#3 The Resilient Woman Story From - From Lady F H

I believe as a result of my childhood trauma, escaping from an abusive marriage after fifteen years, suffering episodes of depression for over 20 years, including losing both my parents and twin sister to death, having endured adversity, and having the capacity to bounce back after being knocked down, has helped me to develop mental toughness and a stronger personality of resilience.

Throughout my life, I have had to deal with some major challenges, setbacks, and unfavourable situations, which have thrown me off guard and caused me to question my existence as a person.

Throughout the process of going through my challenges, I have always told myself, "that no matter what life throws at me, giving up for me was never an option, no matter how frightening and daunting the place I found myself in was." Despite the challenges, I would always try to find a solution by dealing with my problems rationally and questioning myself, taking a step back always, and looking at the problem from another perspective, including journaling which helped me to get my thoughts out of my head and unto paper.

Another thing that really helped me to become more resilient is having a relationship with God and knowing that God loves me and I am not on my own. I belong to God, which gives me a living hope and assurance. This knowing is such a real light-bulb moment for me. For me to develop resilience, I had to make a decision not to let my experiences define me because I am not my trauma, I am not the abuse suffered in my marriage, neither am I the depression experienced. These are just experiences which do not belong to me, to understand that I am not my experiences, i.e., it is so liberating and freeing.

Lastly, having a good solid network of people around me, such as my family and friends, has also been my major contributor to making me a person of resilience, with the ability to endure any adversity, including believing in me and my strength goes a very long way.

I believe having the ability to bounce back and find my inner strength after experiencing childhood trauma, involving physical and emotional abuse, including neglect as a result of the traumatic experiences that I have encountered throughout the journey of my life, has made me a more resilient person. I know I have now developed the ability to bounce back despite my challenges as a person that has endured some very dark, tough moments in life.

#4 The Resilient Woman Perspective From - Master DD

My viewpoints on a resilient woman: Resilience is the ability to withstand pressure when faced with life's challenges, bounce back from adversity and exhibit inner-strength against all odds. On account of the above definition, the following are my summaries of a resilient Woman:

1. Being able to persevere in the face of adversity and difficulties. Hannah in the Bible was childless, for which she was taunted. She never gave up hope and persevered until God blessed her with her first child Samuel who became a prophet.

2. Consistently stands for what is right irrespective of circumstances. The biblical character Ruth is a perfect example.

3. God-dependent - a resilient woman who relies on God for her sustenance and strength - Ruth the Moabite was a good example of unwavering faith bravery. Despite being widowed at a young age, she stuck with her mother-in-law, believing and trusting God that He would make a way.

4. Rachel patiently waited to marry her love Jacob after being cruelly deceived by her father, who tricked Jacob into marrying her sister Leah. Her prayers were answered, and although she was childless at first, she became the mother to Joseph and Benjamin.

5. Courageous: Great courage was exemplified by Queen Esther

when she told the Persian king about a plan to assassinate him, and later, a plan to have all the Jews in Persia killed. Esther combined the power of prayer and bravery and saved her people. From the above examples of resilient female biblical characters, it is evident that the ultimate source of resilience is God. The above examples also highlight the fact that resilience requires conscious and purposive efforts to overcome setbacks by bouncing back from them and becoming a better version of ourselves.

Drawing from the examples above as well as my daily interactions with women both from the personal and professional spheres, I would like to state my experience with resilient women as follows:

1. They keep going irrespective of whatever challenge, obstacle, or distraction is thrown in their path.

2. Resilient women are focused on the bigger picture, and this is what keeps them going.

3. Resilient women have the courage to come out of relationships that are characterised by domestic abuse and impacting their lives and those of their children. They don't endanger their lives and those of their children by staying in a violent and toxic relationship, just for the "sake of the children." It is never a sign of resilience when a woman stays in a toxic relationship such as described above.

4. Resilient women don't allow gender stereotyping, to keep them down or stop them from maximising their potential; hence we have seen a gradual increase in women training as doctors and

not just nursing; engineers; architects; space scientists; etc

5. Resilient women are hardworking, diligent, and resourceful - They don't sit down and rely on men for everything. They contribute to the running of the home. This might not necessarily be financial, especially if they are at home looking after young children. Caring for the children, cooking, and cleaning are major contributions that should be celebrated.

6. A resilient woman is one that doesn't give up easily. However, relentlessly pursuing something which is illegal and selfish is not a mark of resilience.

7. My experience of a resilient woman is one that doesn't allow negative comments to kill her confidence.

8. A resilient woman is one with a positive outlook on life and who, despite life's challenges, would remain focused and determined to achieve what they are destined for.

9. A resilient woman is one who is willing to access and make use of resources available to them, such as family members and friends, children; family and children's centres; leisure centres, etc.

10. A resilient woman ensures she maintains a strong support network of family and friends who she can rely upon for practical and emotional support during difficult times.

Although the debate over whether resilience is innate or learned is ongoing, I feel that everyone should try to develop their resilient threshold. We must try to increase our protective factors and minimise the risk factors.

#5 The Resilient Woman Perspective From - Lady C

What makes me resilient? – There was a time when I questioned my Lord, as to why He had to bring me into this life of pain and suffering. This was the response I received according to his word in Isaiah 44:2 **"The Lord said to me, *"He has made me, formed me in the womb of my mother, therefore I should not be afraid, and He will help me, as He has chosen me."***

At that time, I was incredibly young and did not understand what He meant. But what I can never forget is the word: **"DO NOT BE AFRAID."** This word came at a time when I was driven out of my room by my mum to sleep outside on several occasions by. I lived in absolute fear, was always panicking, and was very anxious. This was a very trying period in my life, and I felt stretched on all fronts. I guess this statement from the Lord has stayed with me all my life to date. It has also helped me gain hope and more assurance, which helped me get through the rough time in the past and even now.

Having endured various dynamics of pain in my life, my faith in the Lord has kept me moving no matter what. I believe that He empowers me on a daily basis; therefore, I can face my tomorrow, no matter what comes my way. My determination not to ever give up shows how resilient I have been and become. Through the test and length of time, I have learnt to be strong.

Resilience is my ability to adapt to difficult situations. When I am confronted with the stresses of life, difficult problems, or when past trauma strikes, I can still experience anger, sorrow, and pain, but still able to keep functioning physically, spiritually, and psychologically by resting in God through prayer. However, resilience isn't about putting up with something difficult, suppressing your feelings, or being patient or visualizing issues out on your own. You cannot handle every struggle on your strength. In fact, being able to reach out to others for support is also a key part of being resilient. This was one of the key reasons **"Women of Beautiful Hearts"** was built on; a women's networking group where women are welcome to network together, support, and empower each other.

I have always struggled to reach out for help, but practising resilience in this way has helped me greatly.

To continue living a life of resilience, I have learnt from my many experiences to make a conscious effort to deal with whatever problem I face and intend to bounce back and not fall apart, which is what the enemy is always looking for. However, even if I fall, I harness inner strength through the power of the Holy Spirit that helps me bounce back from the setback. As believers, Resilience means trusting God to see you through the pain. *"Not by might, nor by power, but by the spirit of God."* **Zechariah 4:6**

God is always there to help us, and to strengthen us, to raise us up from whatever challenges, be it a loss of business, an illness, breakups, marriage issues, family issues, issues in ministry, a disaster, or a loved one's death or going through any type of trauma.

I discovered that whenever my resilience is low, I tend to dwell on problems, be victimized by the problems, get myself overwhelmed, or even turn to unhealthy coping mechanisms, which only lead to more issues. Therefore, to continue being resilient as a believer in Christ, I have made my mind up to stay with God to instil his power of strength and help me through my journey here on earth. I know I can't do without Him because I am only human. ***"And we know that God works all things together for the good of those who love Him, who are called according to His purpose."*Romans 8:28**

From experience, I discovered that being Resilient won't make our problems go away. Instead, it helps us overcome or find ways to deal with the problems. Hence, I made up my mind to fight every obstacle. It's never been easy, but the word of God gives me encouragement.

Zerubbabel was encouraged to continue on despite the obstacles he was facing. That same encouragement and statement remains true for me as a child of God today. The scripture in Haggai reads: ***"but now be strong, Zerubbabel' declares the LORD. 'Be strong, Joshua, son of Jozadak, the high priest. Be strong, all you people of the land,' declares the LORD, 'and work. For I am with you,' declares the LORD Almighty. ⁵ 'This is what I covenanted with you when you came out of Egypt. And my Spirit remains among you. Do not fear."***

Being resilient gives me the ability to see past a problem and look up to God when I am in pain; I find reasons for the pain, I learn lessons knowing that anything that happens is not by accident, God has a plan, God's hands are in it, and if I am able to overcome, I will find rest, peace and satisfaction, and be better in handling the next challenge. Being a Counsellor has greatly helped me become more resilient.

There is a reason or purpose behind every problem or challenge.

"If you haven't thought of this, cast your mind to some challenges you have previously encountered, and you found answers or solutions to those problems, you will notice that every problem or challenge in life has caused a great change or growth in you." You get to discover that all things ended up working for good, though it never looked like that before.

The word of God, according to Ephesians 1:11, says: *"having been predestined according to the plan of him who works out everything in obedience with the purpose of his will."*

The book of Acts 17:28 also reminds us that: *"For in Christ Jesus we live, move and have our being."*

I would say, if I was not a believer in Christ, maybe I couldn't have been more resilient. Yes! Probably, I would have given up in life.

As Christians, we can never do it ourselves unless God is in it. We need God at every stage of our lives. If God is our rock, we will not fall but stand tall. I am still standing tall in spite of all the challenges, because I recognize God in my quest to be more resilient and allow him to be God in my situations. **James 1:12 says:** *"Happy or Blessed is the man who perseveres, who endures, under trial, because when he has stood the test, he will receive the crown of life that God has promised to those who love him."*

Resilience has helped me a lot in my years of experience. Thinking of ways to add value to myself was one of my greatest learning curves. Listed below are some of the methods I decided to practice to maintain my resilience in a balanced way.

1. **Getting connected**: Through the years, I have learnt to build

strong and positive relationships with loved ones and friends. If you don't have any, then make good new ones. Establish other important connections by volunteering at a charitable organisation joining a faith-based or social community. This also helps greatly.

2. **Make every day meaningful:** I try my best every now and then to work out at something that gives me a sense of accomplishment and purpose every day.

3. **Learn from past experience**: I love to always do a review to help me identify positive and negative behaviour patterns; in this way, I get to manage any future encounters.

4. **Remain hopeful**: I always remind myself that I can't change the past, but I can always look towards the future.

5. **Taking care of myself:** This was something I struggled with previously. I used to be very busy, running around, trying to sort out people's issues, almost at fault, while I suffered. However, I learnt that I needed to first take care of "ME" to enable me to take care of others. It suddenly occurred to me that my entire "Well Being" was very important.

6. **Be positive**: No matter how ugly a situation might be, I forcefully allow myself to see through deeply, hoping that something positive will come out of that situation.

I will conclude by saying this: "*let us keep being resilient, working hard, refusing to be intimidated, but through it, all, remain hopeful in the Lord and his promises, **for it is God who works in us, both to will and to do for his good pleasure.**"*Philippians 2:12–13.

#6 The Resilient Woman Story & Perspective From - Lady J S Oluwalana

In answer to this question about what makes someone resilient?

I would like to mention three things that I found helpful for me, in relation to resilience, and the challenges in particular, which I experienced, as follows:

When I was going through my season of singleness, I found this very challenging, especially as a believer, who was trying to be, aiming to be, striving to be exemplary and reflective of my relationship with Jesus Christ, in a way that people can look up to you, and say: "you know what, that's how to go through" or "that's how to enjoy being single," until the man of God comes.

That was indeed a great challenge that stretched me emotionally, but also, that was the time in which I established my relationship with the Lord; so definitely a relationship with Jesus Christ, demonstrated through reading the word daily, having daily worship time, practicing the word, teaching the word, getting involved in discipleship; those basic things has helped me greatly, particularly when there are certain scriptures brought to your attention through other people, especially in prayer meetings, or listening to the word on Sundays.

I noticed how resilient I became when I had a recent experience of stress and anxiety related to the way I was handling all the different roles in my life. I felt burdened and overwhelmed; I also found myself going back to basics. What I mean is that, even though I thought I was doing great, things started going the complete opposite; Therefore, I immediately began to identify different forms of help. I feel that asking for help is sometimes perceived as a sign of weakness, and really that's not always the case. It's actually a sign of growth in resilience. We need to realise that it is only in a few situations that we are able to help ourselves. The majority of situations we encounter might require a very big help from others. There are some situations where one becomes so incapacitated that if one does not use their voice to call out for help, the situation leaves them in a complete mess. I realised calling out for help is better than drowning in that situation.

So for me, I think recognising that you know what, I need help to overcome this situation is a vital thing, and realising and knowing that this is temporary, or this is a season, and I will come through it. For me, that has really helped a great deal. Also, knowing that, "you know what, I have been somewhere like this before, the way I'm feeling, it feels like, wow! Will this feeling ever go away?" However, I know from experience that reminding yourself of what the Lord has done beforehand, or what you did in a previous situation, those things also really do help. It also helps you just to guard yourself up and just for you to know that whatever you are going through, you will come out in that season of waiting.

Again, I just think it's a little by little process; sometimes, you just have to simplify the things that you need to do; ask yourself the question: what are the things that I can do myself?

Do I have the capacity to do those things based on my mental capacity at that time?

I feel this is a vital thought, because sometimes, we often have a lot of burdens, and I think that goes on to other things. For example, on many occasions, we have heard about the woman in Proverbs 31, on how much she did for her family, how well known and respected she was in her community. This scripture is sometimes used as an encouragement when praying for women. It is also used as a yardstick sometimes to measure how other women operate. Again, it is often referred to when some people talk about resilience.

Sometimes, as a woman, I feel like you have to take on so much, especially when people bring up other people as an example; you feel like you have to repeat the kind of things that that person is doing. It is true that you want to do so much and even much better.

However, part of that doing is realising your limitations and how far you can push things. Jesus recognises limitation. He is the saviour of the whole world, yet he said:" is better that I go, and when I go, the Holy Spirit will come, and then you will know that you'll be able to do everything here, to achieve what he has achieved, and still have more to achieve by being on the earth. It wasn't until He went and the Holy Spirit came that they now blew out, and there was an overflow of millions of Christians around the world.

So, I think in the same way, we have to recognise our limitations; as much as we have the Holy Spirit, we're still one person, we are still flesh and blood, and the way we are able to do more is by affecting lives. Also, I think there's a wisdom that we need to address that whilst there is pressure, we need to be sensitive enough to know that not all pressure is from God, some pressure is external, the pressure that people have put on you; and it's up to you to decide whether you want to receive that or shield it.

Another thing that helps me be resilient is that you have to find your balance. When I say to find your own balance, I mean you are pushing yourself, you're making sure that: "ok no, I don't want to be too comfortable here; let me push myself, but you're not pushing yourself beyond what you can manage. You are pushing yourself, but you are doing little by little, making progress little by little, and then, when you look back, you will see how far you have come. You are not measuring yourself by anybody else except Christ. But even there, you have to do it little by little. Let's not forget that the Lord is looking at our hearts. Yes, the deeds are there, but really, it's our hearts that will make our deeds effective and acceptable in his sight.

Out of those things, just to reiterate what has helped me with resilience:

1. My relationship with Christ, through the basic activities of living a lifestyle of worship.

2. Asking for help and finding where those sources of help are, where it is appropriate.

3. Knowing that Seasons come and go, that the situation will not remain, it's not permanent, and even in situations like death, though this too is not permanent, the way that one is feeling during those times are bound to change. It does not remain the same. There are still ways to cope by taking small steps.

Chapter Six

THE RESILIENT WOMAN IN SUMMARY

T he resilient woman, who endures years of mockery, stigma and finger pointing from her community, sometimes friends, and also her family members, as a result of infertility. Amidst all odds, she decides not to give up, maybe attempt the IVF process with several attempts added with faith and perseverance, and end up with a child of her own, or in some cases, more than happy to go through the adoption or fostering route.

The resilient woman, a mother who survives the challenges of raising her children as a result of being divorced, separated, or widowed. Do we ever think about how they get through the school runs, be it a stay at home or a working mum, the normal routines of providing for the family single-handedly, sorting out bills, being there emotionally and socially for her children, and sometimes having to deal with the behaviour of her children in the midst of it all.

The resilient woman is a mother who constantly stands in the gap for her troubled child or children regardless of the pain and disgrace caused by her child's or children's actions. The stigma and labelling she gets from the society when her child is being held as an offender of a crime, awaiting prosecution or already in prison, or in a worst-case scenario, being murdered, going through the grieving process, a mother whose child or children are facing mental health challenges, a mother, whose child is facing addiction of any type. How does she get past putting unnecessary blame on herself and others?

The resilient woman, a mother with a "Special Needs Child" or an "Autistic Child," who despite the challenges faced with the daily dealings and juggling of life, to the point of feeling like you do not have a life on your own, especially in places where less help is available, or even when help is available, the thought of dealing with the emotional, physical, financial and psychological aspects of living with children in need, not forgetting the stigma attached to such due to ignorance and lack of awareness especially if one is living amongst the B.A.M.E community. She tries her best to fight for all the rights entitled to her child, to ensure her child feels valued like every other human being is valued on this planet earth. She proudly showcases her child, their skills, and talents despite their needs. She never gives up! That is resilience right there.

The resilient mother, who despite classing herself as a super mum, can still recognise her struggles and decide to seek help and support from others around her or any formal entity. That same woman then decides to get involved in the lives of others in order to support them with their struggles as a result of her own life's experiences.

The resilient woman, who identifies her limitations and boundaries, decides her place in line with her capabilities and strengths. She also learns to manage her expectations and that of others about her as she goes through life's processes.

The resilient woman who survives in the works of ministry where some women are still struggling to thrive, despite their conviction of being called to actively serve in the faith, amidst isolation and deprivation by some religious aristocrats, who still hold on firmly to the idea that women are not allowed in the forefront of ministry.

On and offline, the resilient woman who also deals with bullying for following her passion as a politician, an arena that is mostly dominated by males.

The resilient woman, a professional working mother, who fights against her employer's decision not to give her flexible hours, allowing her to look after her younger children, due to the fact that childcare costs these days are so expensive that mothers are prepared to stay at home with their children. Such mothers love their profession and would not want to jeopardize family life at such an early stage. Other mothers, who face similar situations, will normally take a drastic decision to resign from their jobs for a while until their young ones have passed early developmental stages. Then, they will start again, firstly with a part-time role, until they make a decision to go back full time.

The resilient woman never allows anything to deter her from believing and, again, lobbying alongside her peers for equal pay or salary in the work place. Gone are the days when the "status Co" took ages to shift, from the traditional mindset that there were only certain types of jobs that women could do. We now live in the 21st Century, and yet still, women are fighting for equal pay, as a lot of them have been tested and proven that, not only do they do some of the jobs that men do, they are also very excellent at that same job, some women have even attained higher ranking than men in some employment hierarchy. This particular topic is very prevalent around nations today, so I want to take a guess that we are not ignorant of this reality.

The resilient woman, the nursing practitioner in every facet, who never gives up on their patient, even when some days can be very rough, and morally low, either because of the loss of lives they have cared for, or working extra long hours due to staff shortage, or even when they feel less appreciated by those at the top, sadly even by families of the very patients they care for, yet still they push on. That's resilience right there!

The resilient woman, an activist, who also rallies around for a great cause that affects the less privileged in their communities, who is constantly faced with criticisms and red-tapes, preventing a safe and peaceful way of navigating through systems.

The resilient woman, who fought through abusive relationships to safety, having sacrificed all she laboured for, who decides to kick off the stigma around failed relationships, gets prepared to walk into a new dimension of rebuilding herself, decides to live life, explore and love all over again.

The resilient woman, who overcomes body-shaming by taking her time to love herself the way she is and at the same time working on improving her lifestyle towards a prolonged healthy one.

The resilient woman in business, who spent her last penny to establish her business, to ensure she provides for her children's welfare and education, especially if her family lives in a country where there is no free education. She perseveres despite the uncertainties of the business. Some days, business is great, the sales are excellent; on other days, business does not look like business at all, as the sales just go down. She still finds money to pay her rent and other bills relating to the business. She loses money just when she thought she could build up on the very products she spends money on. Then comes a time when the heavens seem to open, and she then experiences what we describe as" showers of blessing."

The woman in business, who never gives up, whether her business was affected by a national, global, or natural disaster. Whether her goods were looted at the entry port or stolen by thieves, whether it was a disappointment from various vendors and suppliers, she perseveres and continues pushing. Whenever she feels stuck, she is not put off by asking other business colleagues for ideas and assistance. She pushes for her business despite the weather, be it under the rain, sunshine, or cold.

While there might be many more to say about the resilient woman, kindly permit me to take a bow at this juncture. I also feel this might encourage you as readers to add your own lines to what's been said here.

Chapter Seven

INSPIRATIONAL QUOTATIONS ON RESILIENCE

"Resilience is accepting your new reality, even if it's less good than the one you had before. You can fight it, you can do nothing but scream about what you've lost, or you can accept that and try to put together something that's good." — **Elizabeth Edwards**

"My scars remind me that I did indeed survive my deepest wounds. That in itself is an accomplishment. And they bring to mind something else, too. They remind me that the damage life has inflicted on me has, in many places, left me stronger and more resilient. What hurt me in the past has actually made me better equipped to face the present." — **Steve Goodier**

"Everyone has the ability to increase resilience to stress. It requires hard work and dedication, but over time, you can equip yourself to handle whatever life throws your way without adverse effects on your health.

Training your brain to manage stress won't just affect the quality of your life, but perhaps even the length of it." —**Amy Morin**

"It's your reaction to adversity, not adversity itself, that determines how your life's story will develop." —**Dieter F. Uchtdorf**

"Do not judge me by my success, judge me by how many times I fell and got back up again." —**Nelson Mandela**

"No matter how you define success, you will need to be resilient, empowered, authentic, and limber to get there." —**Joanie Connell**

"Rock bottom became the solid foundation on which I rebuilt my life." —**J.K. Rowling**

"When we tackle obstacles, we find hidden reserves of courage and resilience we did not know we had. And it is only when we are faced with failure do we realize that these resources were always there within us. We only need to find them and move on with our lives." —**A.P.J. Abdul Kalam**

"It is really wonderful how much resilience there is in human nature. Let any obstructing cause, no matter what, be removed in any way, even by death, and we fly back to first principles of hope and enjoyment." —**Bram Stoker**

Indeed, this life is a test. It is a test of many things – of our convictions and priorities, our faith and our faithfulness, our patience and our resilience, and in the end, our ultimate desires." —**Sheri L.**

Encouraging Biblical Quotations on Resilience

"I am able to do all things through Him who strengthens me." — **Philippians 4:13**

"Be on your guard; stand firm in the faith; be courageous; be strong." —**1 Corinthians 16:13**

"So do not fear, for I am with you; do not be dismayed, for I am your God. I will strengthen you and help you; I will uphold you with my righteous right hand."—**Isaiah 41:10**

"Stand firm, and you will win life."—**Luke 21:19**

"We are afflicted in every way, but not crushed; perplexed, but not driven to despair; persecuted, but not forsaken; struck down, but not destroyed." —**2 Corinthians 4:8-9**

"Blessed is the one who perseveres under trial because, having stood the test, that person will receive the crown of life that the Lord has promised to those who love him." —**James 1:12**

"⁷ I have fought the good fight, I have finished the race, I have kept the faith. ⁸ Now there is in store for me the crown of righteousness, which the Lord, the righteous Judge, will award to me on that day—and not only to me, but also to all who have longed for his appearing." —**2 Timothy 4:7-8**

Appreciations

Firstly, I would like to thank my Lord and the Holy Spirit for his tremendous strength and grace over my life. I always wonder how I do it. Nothing but his grace for me!

Secondly, I would also like to extend my appreciation to Pastor Boomy Tokan, always wanting to see me progress, an Encourager and Motivator, Mentor, and Coach. The moment he messaged me about expanding this topic of resilience, it became a clear confirmation of the witness I had after my Mother's Day ministration.

Next is to extend my heartfelt thanks to all who participated with their various stories and perspectives on resilience; Lady Pastor Oyinlola Bukky Akande, Lady C, Lady J S Oluwalana, Lady FH, master BT, and Master DD. Your contribution has made a huge difference and I believe will be to those who read the book.

My appreciation also goes to my Editors and Designer for all their hard-work towards the publication of this book.

Finally, to all who have prayed for me, supported me in various ways towards ministry and the various things I do, I want to say thank you!

May my Lord continue to bless you all richly!

CONTRIBUTORS

Oyinlola Bukky Akande is a Life-Coach, Speaker, Author, Publisher, Opportunity Broker, Bridge Builder, Network Marketer, and Event Co-ordinator. She has served in the Retail & Sales industry, and her experience spans over 25 years. OBA's lengthy experience and refined interpersonal skills have made her a customer service expert. She has authored three books titled "Diary of the Unique Woman," "The Life Wires Coupons," & "Hello, I am Pleased to Meet You."

OBA has also co-authored and published two books titled 'Unique Insights' & 'Unique Foresight's.' She is the *President* of Unique Women International and runs a women's only mentor-ship group called Unique Legacy. The heart of Unique Legacy is to aid the development of ideas of women, young women and connect them with professionals in their industry or field. Co-Founder of Rapha Nurturing Academy. OBA is a Certified CBT Trainer; she holds a BSC in Events Management. She is a Co-Pastor of Shalom Life Changers Ministry and married to Kenny Akande, senior Pastor of Shalom Life Changers, and they are blessed with children.

Lady J S Oluwalana

Author of "Shouldn't I Be Married By Now?" A prayer guide with stories for single Christian women.

Buy My First Book!

Don't Judge Me: I Am A Single Parent

Click Here: https://amzn.to/3sTf31P

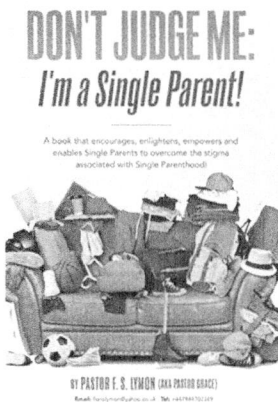

REFERENCES

1. Scriptures from The New International Version.

2. Miriam Webster Dictionary.

3. The "Very Well Mind" Article by Kendra Cherry, updated on the 24th of April 2021.

4. The American Psychological Association publication, updated on 1st of February 2020.

5. "Everyday Health.com," reviewed on 11th December 2020.

6. *The Journal of Gerontology* Research published in April 2016.

7. The *Ecology and Society* journal, published in 2015.

8. The Counselling Directory UK, Joshua Miles response; published on the 15th of May 2015.

Printed in Great Britain
by Amazon